Living The Life You Taught Me

(Unforgettable Memoirs)

Veloisa Diana Simpson

with Misha McConnell-Todman

Published and Distributed by:
Professional Publishing House
1425 W. Manchester Ave., Suite B
Los Angeles, California 90047
www.professionalpublishinghouse.com
Drrosie@aol.com
(323) 750-3592

Cover design: Misha McConnell-Todman
Cover layout: Jay De Vance, III
First printing: August 2012
ISBN:978-0-9853259-6-1
10987654321

TABLE OF CONTENTS

ABOUT THE AUTHOR

Veloisa Diana Simpson was born in Indianapolis, Indiana. As early as 10 years of age, she attended Phyllis Wheatley Y.W.C.A. where her natural and gifted dancing talents were discovered. Veloisa's interest and participation continued to grow in Y.W.C.A. and the Girls Scouts. After completing Crispus Attucks High School, Veloisa entered West Virginia State University, where she had high ambitions of becoming a professional ballerina. This marked the beginning of a most interesting chain of events.

Besides appearing in every dance production on campus, Veloisa appeared on the front cover of colored magazines, which led to an audition and invitation for "New Faces," a touring musical. Veloisa's mother felt it best that her daughter (an only child) decline this offer.

Respecting her mother's wishes, she declined and continued her schooling, graduating with a Bachelor of <u>Science</u> in Education. The following 10 years, Veloisa taught students at Robert Gould Shaw Elementary School. She decided to move to California to start a new chapter in her life.

Veloisa is a member of Alpha Kappa Alpha (AKA) Sorority, Inc. and Life Member of Theta Mu Omega Chapter of Inglewood, California. She holds a Bachelor of Arts Degree in Education from West Virginia State University and a Master of Science Degree in Education from California Lutheran University. After fulfilling her educational accomplishments, she became employed as a Special Education Teacher for the Compton Unified School District (CUSD). Veloisa retired in 1986 from the CUSD. She was honored with a Certificate of Meritorious Service for 27 years of an outstanding contribution and service to CUSD students, staff, and community.

Special Achievements:

Veloisa received recognition for outstanding classroom technique in "Behavior Modification," Certificate of Participation in fields testing the Social Learning Curriculum from Research and Development Center

Mental Retardation at Yeshiva University and awarded outstanding Teacher of the Year (Parents and Students Relationship).

The Marquis, "Who's Who Publications Board" certifies that Veloisa Diana Simpson is one of the subjects listed in *Who's Who Biographical Record Child Development Professional*, First Edition—inclusion in which is limited to those individuals who have demonstrated professional competence in their fields of endeavor and who thereby contributed significantly to the betterment of contemporary society.

Veloisa has written several articles in magazines for Special Education Teachers. In 1991, she received a Certificate of Appreciation for Reading is Fundamental (RIF) for Outstanding and Dedicated Service to the boys and girls of Raymond Avenue Elementary School in Los Angeles, California.

PREFACE

Why...Writing the Story of my Life

I am writing the story of my life. When I read a book or an article, I often read a story of someone's life experience. People suffer losses, celebrate victories and make life-changing decisions. As I read the material, I learn from their stories. In the same way, I want to tell my story by the way I lived and by the choices I've made and continue to make. My story may be one of courage, kindness, or creativity, or perhaps my life will inspire others to a greater achievement.

Each day, I add a page to my story. If I want to begin a fresh chapter, I am free to begin anew. I begin each day eager to see what will happen on this page of my journey. My entire family has transitioned to Heaven, so I am all alone. I am walking with God in my Heart. I believe God has blessed me with a special gift.

I am a unique creation of a loving God. My individuality is a gift from God. Such a gift allows me the freedom to explore my thoughts and feelings, and then to live my life the best way that I know how. I can recognize what is right for me. I know that being a unique individual I am moving toward my greater potential. God has blessed me with the gift of "individuality."

As we get older, we say good-bye to many people that we have encountered at some point in our lives. We bid farewell to our friends and discover our capacity to love and communicate and have intimacy—real intimacy, not superficial intimacy—that we had during our youthful days.

Two questions that I ask of myself:
1. Did I learn to live wisely?
2. Did I love well?

Answer:
1. Absolutely!
2. Oh YES!

DEDICATION TO MY MOTHER

(Lillian E. Lewis)

$\mathcal{I}$dedicate this book to my mother, Lillian Elizabeth Lewis.

Mother, you were my strength when I was weak and a great source of light when times were dark. Because of you, I have developed into the person that I am. I am able to do the things that I do. Mother, words cannot describe how much I miss seeing you, having our lengthy home and phone conversations. To me, that seemed timeless, and simply knowing that you were there for me.

After seeing or phoning my mother, I would say, "See you later, alligator." Then, my mother would say, "After while, crocodile."

Mother, I never realized how much you taught me.
I am very grateful that you gave me the gift of life.
The three "Ls" you taught me are important in my life:

11

Look *and you will see…*
Listen *and you will hear…*
Love *and you will live...*
    You told me to challenge myself and to be considerate of others. These are lessons that I treasure. I love and miss you dearly.

    Your beloved daughter,
    Veloisa Diana Simpson

※

Taking my mother's advice, she went through so much in her life, yet always managed to come out in a very positive way. She really managed to have a very happy life and give me just an amazing childhood. My mother always helped people find a way to get through the day and their own lives in a positive way. She did that until she passed away at the age of 104 years old. I learned from her that if your heart is open, you could let go of your pain.

You can let go of things that you or someone else said or did, bad circumstances that happened and find a way to process it and move forward. Life is full of challenges, and that's what life is. It's a big ol' lovely roller coaster of ups and downs. I think if you hang on to pain or resentment, it will eat you up alive!

Veloisa Diana Simpson

This is a tribute for you, Mother, with love and thanks for being all the special things that you were to me… "See you later, alligator."

"My mother's heart was a beautiful heart with limitless love for sharing. A heart filled with the bright, shining gifts of her warm understanding and caring. My mother's heart was a generous heart that found its true joy in sensing the needs of the people around her, and adding richness to living. My mother's heart was a wise, gentle heart that saw only goodness in others; no wonder I know deep within my own heart. She was the sweetest and best of all mothers."

Always my love ~ your daughter,
Veloisa Diana

Living the Life You Taught Me

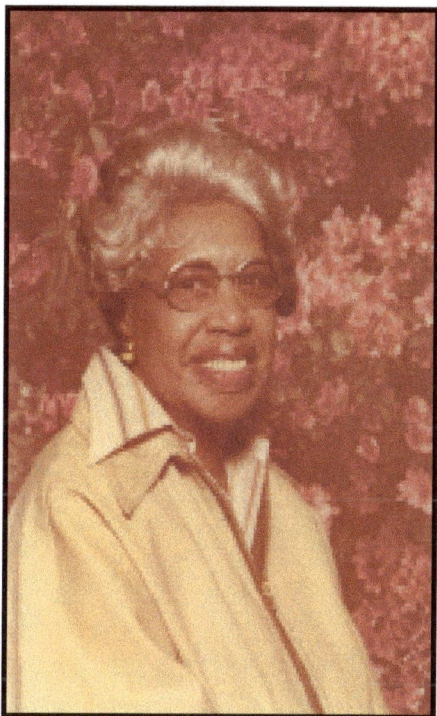

Lillian Elizabeth Lewis (104 years old)

Sunrise: July 29, 1905

Sunset: January 1, 2010

ACKNOWLEDGEMENTS

*A*ssociated friends…there isn't enough space to individually acknowledge. Please know that in my heart, I am grateful and blessed to have had your friendship.
(You know who you are) SMILE!!!

A SPECIAL THANKS to all of the people (assorted nuts) who played a significant role in my life:

1. Nancy Johnson (Mosquito)
2. Deni Pavon (Angel)
3. Catherine McCarns-Johnson (Precious)
4. Kim Jackson (Sunshine), my Godchild
5. Misha McConnell-Todman (Turtle Dove)
6. Billie Barrett (Ringing Bell)

7. Sharron Williams (Firecracker)

8. Lillian R. Pope (Dreamer), deceased ~ I Miss You!!

Thank you, Veloisa Diana Simpson (The Squirrel)

A special thanks to Misha McConnell-Todman for all her hours of help on this book. In addition to Cathy McCarns-Johnson for her treasured assistance.

COLONOSCOPY TESTS

Years 2002 & 2010

In April 2002, I went in for a colonoscopy test. My doctors had their findings, and I was diagnosed with colon cancer. When they told me their findings, I cried and I yelled, and I was simply hysterical. This could not have been happening to me, but it was, and surgery to remove the tumor was scheduled.

On the eve of the surgery, I spent the night praying and having a conversation with God. I was picked up the next morning for surgery. My mother and friends were smiling saying, "Everything is going to be all right," as I was rolled off into the operating room. The surgery went well, and I was elated.

I have had two serious surgeries (both for colon cancer) in my life, so I know pain and fear. I do not fear death. Dying is easy. Living is hard work. I clearly realize that our bodies are not who we are. Although, while we are in our bodies, we definitely need to take care of them. It's kind of like a car. If you don't take care of it, it doesn't run very well.

Dear Doctors
Steven A. Lerner, Robert M. Shorr, and Craig M. Smith

Although the years 2002 and 2010 had been filled with many challenges, my trials were greatly lightened by your brilliant minds and skillful hands. I pray that you continue to be showered with God's richest blessings!!

Sincerely with love,
Veloisa Diana Simpson

LETTERS TO GOD

2002 Surgery

Heavenly Father,

The road ahead looks very short and I feel that I am about to reach its end. Yet, I know that every sunset is followed by a sunrise, and death is always the prelude to resurrection. Maybe this isn't the end of the road after all! Maybe, just maybe, it's a bend in the road. I AM PRAYING!

Love,

Veloisa Diana

ನಲ

Heavenly Father,

Wonderful things are happening in my heart this very moment, Oh God. The heavy stone that entombed a dead joy is rolling away and the joy is coming alive again. There is light breaking through the crack in the hardened walls around my soul. Oh God, this is a day to rejoice…I am in REMISSION.

I Love You,
Veloisa Diana Simpson

৩৩

Heavenly Father,

I know that you have shown me that there is no gain without pain. Well Lord, I must really be making headway because I hurt, hurt, hurt. However, I know if I will keep faith and if You will give the power that together, we will WIN.

Love Your Child,
Veloisa Diana Simpson

৩৩

Heavenly Father,

I thank you for loving me. Loving Father, touch me with Your healing hands. My mind and emotions, even the deepest recess of my heart. Saturate my entire being with Your presence, love, joy, and peace. Draw me ever closer to Your every moment of my life. Father, You are the highest of my eyes. The thrills in my body and the sweet sounds in my ears and in my heart."

Your Lovely Child,

Veloisa Diana Simpson

࿚

Heavenly Father,

Thank you that I am alive with eyes to see the brightness of a new day; the ears to hear every sound. I thank God that You have created me to be a unique, special, and different human being. There has never been and there will never be another exactly like me. You have a special plan just for me, a mission that only I can fulfill.

Thank you,

Veloisa Diana Simpson

࿚

Veloisa Diana Simpson

2011 Remission

Heavenly Father,

It is because of You that I am able to look forward with anticipation, knowing that You have prepared me for tomorrow. I come now so thankful for the beautiful chapters and for the happy endings that I cannot even imagine.

Your Lovely Child,
Veloisa Diana Simpson

ༀ

Heavenly Father,

I have this vision for tomorrow. My tomorrow ultimately will be free of fears. My tomorrow will be controlled by faith and in my tomorrow You will be by my side. I know that nothing is impossible with all of my tomorrows in Your hands."

Love,
Veloisa Diana Simpson

HEALING

Coping is 99% attitude. People are always complimenting me, saying things like, "You look terrific! You are amazing!" And my all-time favorite is "You don't look like you have had cancer!" Having been diagnosed with colon cancer in April 2002, transitioned into remission up to the year of 2010, a cancer section was detected. Surgery was performed again. My "Dream-Team" Doctors are saying they got it all this time.

Every three months they draw blood. New medications are making breakthroughs all the time in the battle against cancer. As much as I appreciated these encouraging words, I can honestly say that coping is really 99% attitude. I didn't lose my hair (its a little thinner). Considering all things, I do look terrific, and I am amazing. So what's the secret? Having faith and hope.

Whether I am desiring a change for the better for my health or in my life in general, or whether life is asking such a change in me, I sometimes wonder how I will get from where I am to where I want to be. I know this; I don't have to do it all alone, and I certainly don't have to do it all at once!

The first step, however small, creates momentum. Taking the first step relieves any self-doubt and builds my confidence. The next one is a little easier, and before I know it, I have made tremendous progress on a whole new path of better living. I make a commitment to take one-step at a time. I move step-by-step in being a healthier, happier me.

Surviving the surgery and being in remission from colon cancer, I try never to take anything about my body for granted. I certainly want to ensure that my bones are strong and supportive. I maintain a good practice by including foods that contain calcium in my daily meals. Also, exercising properly helps maintain and rebuild my bones. So I make it a point to eat right and follow a routine of exercises that fit my needs and lifestyle.

Healing from colon cancer (remission), there is a very essence of divine light within me that heals me at a depth. The Christ Spirit is healing energy that radiates powerfully within my inner cell and atom, and renews my every organ and tissue. The appearance of darkness, the light of Christ continually shines within me. If there ever is an appearance of a need for healing, I affirm that the Spirit of Christ within is shining brightly and healing me in every needed way.

In sweet moments of prayer, I give total attention of the Christ Spirit that is renewing me with energy and enthusiasm for life. I give thanks for health and wholeness of mind and body. It's true; I may often express a desire to change something about myself; the way I look or the way I act.

Making changes in my lifestyle in order to improve my health or the quality of my life can benefit me greatly. But, I remember not to overlook one very important fact. I am a wonderful and complete person, just as I am.

It is great to be alive, and it is a blessing to be able to recognize the worthiness and completeness of myself and everyone around me. My understanding of self-worth and appreciation for others are healing practices that promote health in my body and a satisfaction within my soul.

I may think of pain as anything but something positive, but I know that it is the very nature of pain to alert me that my body needs added care or healing. Pain is my wake-up call to greater health. If I am experiencing pain from a tension headache to an upset stomach or an aching back, my body is definitely sending out a wake-up call. This is a strong indication that something needs to be addressed. Prayer takes the fear out of what I am experiencing and can even relieve the pain.

The Christ within me expresses health and vitality in mind and body, holding only the highest thoughts of strength and vitality. I make positive statements about my health. I know that through the Christ Spirit within, I am whole, well, and free. With faith in the renewing power of Christ, I speak life-affirming words. My thoughts and words work together with renewing to strengthen my mind and body. I willingly accept making healthy choices and following strengthening routines that promote greater well-being and energy.

When I am caught up in a troubled relationship or concerned about an illness, healing may seem to be a distant dream. However, by releasing my hold on the issue, I can feel my consciousness begin to shift. I center myself in the "Divine Lane" and remember that I was created in the likeness of God. As God's beloved expression, I give no power to disease, strife, or unrest in my life. I release any barrier to the life-giving energy that flows through my body, my relationships, and me. I open to God's healing presence. I feel God's love radiate within me, revitalizing my body and my life with health and harmony. I witness transformation, body and soul.

I am refreshed and renewed in my mind, body, and spirit. When I think about my health and the way I approach it, I ask myself if I am doing all I need to do to be healthy, whole, and well. If I can do more, I take this opportunity to refresh and perhaps adapt new healthy habits. Such as, initiate exercising more to help me get in tune with my body. Of the many healthy practices available to me, I follow my inner guidance and find which ones are right for me. I am refreshed and renewed in mind, body, and spirit.

My diagnosis was kind of a wake-up call. When something like this happens, you begin to think what it all means. I have always been grateful for family and for all that I have been given, but I realized it is something deeper than that. It is just a realization of how things can change in a moment. So having cancer does make you try to be better at everything you do and enjoy every moment.

I avail myself of every opportunity for growth and service by keeping my mind open and my soul receptive. I do not shrink from challenge or new adventures. Every opportunity finds me eager and ready to serve in larger, more generous ways. I open the door of my mind to divine understanding, the door to my heart to divine love and presence. I let the Spirit of God flow through me, as I exercise an active role in the world around me. Releasing any limiting thoughts, I listen and learn.

Living Now. I live in the now…a time of spiritual growth and discovery. Although, I may have plans for the future, for my special dreams and goals, I realize that right now, at this very moment, is the time frame in which I live. How important it is to live each day, each moment knowing I am one with God and one with the Spirit of God within others.

This understanding satisfied that I am not continually wanting more things or rushing to complete some project. I am living in the now, affirming that each moment I can begin anew. If I was disappointed in myself or someone else yesterday, I take heart for today is a new beginning for us all. And the beauty of living in the now is discovering so much more of God in me and God is my world.

I speak words of peace, inspiration and hope. The words I speak or write contain immense creative power. I confidently state my goals or intentions. I set in motion ideas that have the power to manifest in my life. At the same time, sharing uplifting words has a positive impact on others. Words of kindness and caring create a healing and nurturing environment. Because the words I use have such power, I choose them carefully, taking time in prayer before speaking or writing them. My words create peace where there was discord, inspiration, where there was apathy, and hope where there was despair. I share words that bless and uplift.

I am alive, alert, and enthusiastic about life! My mind and body are in an ongoing conversation. My body responds to my thoughts, and my mind continually receives messages from my body, especially when something is out of order. However, I am more than a body. I am created in the image and likeness of God. As I bring my spiritual awareness into the conversation between mind and body,

I keep myself in balance. With food and water, rest and exercise, I send an affirmation of life and renewal to every cell of my being. With spirit-centered thoughts, words and actions, I claim my true identity as a whole and healthy expression of God, mind, body, and spirit.

LIVING WITH FAITH AND HOPE

There is a place in my home that I call The Resource Room. I pray in this room, thanking God for awakening me. There's a chain to turn on the light. On the chain is the word HOPE, which was sent to me from Marlo Thomas. Going through chemo treatment, I am a longtime supporter of St. Jude Children's Hospital. I believe in hope and faith. With hope one can *think*, one can *work*, and one can *dream*. If you have hope, you have *everything*. Faith is the strength of the soul inside. I release every concern and move forward with faith. I used to tell my mother about various health examinations that I had to take. My mother could obviously see that I was worrying.

Today, I choose to refrain from worry and live in faith. Faith is opposite of worry. For faith allows me to let go of what is troubling me and release it to God. Through faith in God, I experience the joy of the present moment. Through faith in God, I am free from stress or concern. I cannot predict what will happen to me on any given day, but I can make the choice to be positive and worry-free. By doing so, I move forward in faith, living in the moment and trusting God for the right outcomes.

Any darkness of doubt abilities dissolves in a powerful light of truth. I affirm the following with assurance: I believe in myself. I trust myself because I have faith and hope with the Spirit of God within me. There is every reason to believe in trust and value myself, because the love, faith, and hope within me. I know this for myself and for all others. I live with enthusiasm and purpose. I am celebrating every moment of living with joy and thanksgiving.

I have recognized that worry thoughts are stumbling blocks on my way toward achievements. Consequently, if I worry that something is going to be difficult it likely will be. So I open to the underlying potential in what might seem to be a difficulty. I know that all matters can be handled with ease as I let faith within express through me in wise and wonderful ways. I can do what is mine to do and do it well. I am neither timid nor boastful. A feeling of ease fortified by my awareness of my innate divinity nudges me along from thinking to planning to doing. From my inner sacred reservoir, I call on wisdom and understanding life and vigor to move me forward in both simple and complex activities.

Every one person has a purpose. I may discover mine when troubled by a situation and feel called to be a part of the situation. The path may not be perfectly clear. I may not know what action to take. Nevertheless, I begin right where I am. I trust my inner wisdom to show me the way. Rather than worry about making a mistake, I pray and take a small step, trusting that God will place a lamp before my feet, guiding me as I go. As I give of myself in a sacred service, everything I need is provided. I joyfully do what is mine to do. My faith grows even deeper as I give from abundance. As I step out on faith, I am strong.

Faith is a cornerstone in my life, and peace is my experience. I am strengthened by the boldness of my faith. I pray and give thanks for the Christ Spirit that is expressing through me and as me. In strength and with faith, I look directly into a healing challenge and realize the wholeness that awaits expression. I look beyond the appearances of lack and know the abundance is being manifested. Faith is a cornerstone in my life, and peace is my experience in all situations.

Faith is quite different from hope or belief. Hopes can be dashed. Certain beliefs can change or proved wrong. Faith, however, is stronger than either of these. Faith is a deep inner realization of God. At times, I may have a doubt that causes me to seek greater understanding. With this deeper wisdom, I build a deeper faith in God.

The Spirit of God is active in my life at all times and in all situations. Each prayer I pray increases my realization of God. My God awareness supports me as I return my attention to the day and the activities of life. Now even more, I know that I am working with God to co-create a life of wisdom, health, prosperity, and peace.

A little faith goes a long way in clearing our minds, in restoring inner peace, in allowing us to function as people who are capable of great things, for indeed we are. Faith is God in us and others develop courage, patience, understanding, and every aspect of our lives. Each thought or act of faith is like a single fiber that when woven with others, creates a lifeline that connects us to health, peace, prosperity, and great opportunities. I have enough faith. Faith that keeps me going when there seems no way to go on. Such faith is the understanding that God will see me through. Faith is surrendering to God's presence and accepting that without God, nothing is impossible.

Faith comes to us when we cease to think of external things as having power over us; and realize that God, which is all power, brings us. We increase our faith in God as we realize that, in reality, there is only God. No other power exists. I wake up in the mornings in anticipation looking forward to seeing the activity of Spirit in the day ahead. I have faith that the goodness of God is now manifesting in, through, and around me. Approaching every situation from the standpoint of absolute faith in God, I find my worries and doubts short lived. Faith brings answers to prayers, visible and tangible evidence of the goodness of God.

FINDING MY MOTIVATION

New Beginnings. Each moment of my life has the potential to be a new beginning. There are fresh choices to make, new ideas to adopt, new hopes to enliven. My life is under my authority, and I use this power to create the life I choose. At the start of any new venture, I may worry that it will be too hard or wonder whether I will know what to do. How I choose to respond to these worries is up to me.

I choose peace. I choose faith. I choose support from family and friends. I know that I am the very essence of the living, loving God within me. There is a new, wiser, healthier, more peaceful person emerging in my life every day. And what glory I feel in knowing that this new person is the real me! I have been through *turning points* in my lifetime. I overcame fear, changed my way of thinking, found inner reserves of courage and strength. As I look back on these times, I realize I was never alone. God was with me as a guiding and comforting presence, and a strengthening power. This gives me comfort and peace. I give thanks for the turning points in my life. For through them, I have emerged stronger and wiser. I have been blessed with new ideas, new attitudes, and new ways of seeing the world around me and the people in it. What a blessing to know that God is with me in these moments and in every moment of my life!

"This light of mine, I'm gonna let it shine." Looking ahead to any tasks that may lay before me, every thought I think every word I say, every situation I experience is another opportunity for me. Along with life's journey immersed in God's loving presence. I am filled with confidence. I see myself aglow with an inner, divine light. My life is here...let it shine, let it shine!

Being patient is a way I express my love for life. I love life and I know that my love for life helps me to be patient with others and myself. Life is so much more meaningful and interesting when I practice patience. Being patient is a way of practicing good health. I think about how much stress I save my body from going through when I am patient. I truly love the life that God has given me, and being patient is a way I express that love.

Just as I make financial and business commitments in my life, I also make personal commitments to myself each day. In thoughts, word, and action, I keep the commitment to being my best self with all people in all circumstances. I set an intention to let my divine light shine to allow the goodness of God to express through me. I am kind and understanding, gracious and forgiving, looking for the best in everyone and every situation. Spirit supports the fulfillment of my intentions. I act on them with energy and enthusiasm, fulfilling my commitment to be my best self every day.

I notice the good within and around me, and I am blessed. I create my experiences by what I choose to focus on. Holding positive thoughts and releasing negative ones is a powerful way to create a life that blesses me. I focus on my strengths and divine faculties. With each positive thought, I become more aware of the creative power within me.

I live life with intention and seek companions who are joyful and uplifting. I pay attention to beauty of the world around me. I choose to believe in goodness and love. As I take notice of the good within and around me, my life is blessed.

Being strong...I have resolve and resilience to do what is mine to do. Although, difficult circumstances come my way from time to time, I know better than to let outer situations get the best of me. I remember that whatever I am, God is and always will be. A child learning to walk will fall on occasion, but he will also get up and try again. The child gets stronger and steadier with every try; and eventually, walks without effort. Like that child, I have an inner resilience. If I stumble occasionally, I learn and grow from any seeming mistakes or missteps. I have the inner strength to bounce back from any challenges. Knowing this, I move through my day with confidence and flexibility. I have the inner resolve and resilience to do whatever is mine to do.

I am calm and serene. Nothing can disturb me without my permission. For that reason, I begin my day with a choice for peace. Regardless of external events, the length or urgency of my to-do list or the activity of my busy mind, I find peace within. As I become quiet and aware of my thoughts and emotions, I am not sidetracked by any rash reaction to turmoil. I focus my attention on my breathing, close my eyes, and envision the tranquility of Spirit. I am calm, and I make a few simple choices. I SMILE! I listen to the WAVE RADIO station. With the sound of music in Spirit, I am calm, serene, and undisturbed.

Taking charge…I am responsible for my life. With Spirit as my guide, I take charge of my life. I have all I need to create the life I desire through the power and guidance of Spirit within me. I take charge of my health by affirming the truth of my being. I am whole and perfect, physically, and spiritually beautiful. Next, I take action in support of this truth by getting sufficient rest, exercising, and eating a balanced diet. I take charge of my attitude by associating with people who are positive and uplifting and by looking for the best in others and myself. I take charge of my success by accepting responsibility for my life and acting upon the wisdom of Spirit within me. I take charge of my life by using the gifts of Spirit in life, enhancing ways. Spirit is my guide, as I create the life I desire.

Believing that my prosperity is measured only by the money in my bank account may leave me feeling vulnerable and concerned about scarcity and lack. But prosperity is not the possession of things, rather recognition of divine supply. Prosperity means many things to many people. To some, prosperity means employment, to others a home, and to others money in the bank.

Life is meant to be lived abundantly rather than focusing on lack. I acknowledge the ways in which I am blessed. I acknowledge the prosperity already evident in my life. I open my mind and heart to the abundance that is already here. I do my part to open the way for greater prosperity to manifest. I have everything I need today, tomorrow, and always.

I release and let go, ready to make the most of this present moment. As I reflect on the events of the past years, I recognize successes and failures, gains, and losses. Each event has taught me something and made me wiser. Knowing this, I acknowledge and release the past years in gratitude. In contemplation of the coming years, whether I am excited or apprehensive, I know the Spirit of God will empower me to meet every situation with confidence and strength. I release any concerns I may have about the future. I am ready to stand tall in this present moment. I appreciate the now, perfectly balanced between the blessings of the past and the promise of the future.

I open my mind and heart to new understanding. I have had instances in my life that were "aha" moments, flashes of insight when I suddenly understood a particular idea or concept. It was as if a light bulb went off, and I knew what I needed to know. Spiritual growth can be filled with these moments of deep understanding, when I know at a soul level that I am one with God.

Just as a child learns to read one letter at a time, I learn more about my spiritual nature one moment at a time. Whenever or however it may occur, each glimpse of divine wisdom is an opportunity to learn and grow in spiritual understanding and faith. Every "aha" moment with God is part of my ongoing process of spiritual growth, leading me deeper in faith, strengthening my confidence.

Choosing patience I am compassionate and kind. Every day, I have the chance to be cultivated and strengthen any trait I choose. I elect to develop the quality of patience. Co-creating my life I choose to be patient and grow in my understanding that all things happen in their own time. I wait patiently for demonstration to occur in the right place and time. In silence of prayers, I draw patience within me. In dealings with others, I exercise my patience in every conversation and interactions. I approach life with the kindness and compassion that is a natural result of a patient heart and mind.

No matter how many plans I make or how much I prepare for some event, nothing much will come of it, unless I take action. So I make a day for action on my beliefs, a day for stepping out in faith, a day for knocking on the door to new and greater opportunities. I may begin by having an outline of a general plan. Planning helps get my mind focused on what I want or expect, so I plan only for the best! Once I have an outline in mind, I take it to God and prayer. In the sacred atmosphere of prayer, I offer my plan to the Master for any revisions that are needed. I knock on the door to greater opportunity as I let my plans be preliminary ones that are open to divine revisions.

I am a spiritual being living out my true reality. When I truly know who I am, I can live the truth of my reality. I am a spiritual being. So instead of thinking or speaking of myself in terms of weakness or limitation, I think and speak of strength, for I can draw upon the reservoir of spiritual strength that is within me. How can I be sure that it is always there? I can, because I have been created with the Spirit of God within me. When I have decisions to make or a test to complete, I have the wisdom and understanding to do my best. And prayer is part of my preparation for any project, test, or situation. In times of prayer, I gain new insight into the real me, the spiritual being that is capable, loving, peaceful, and ready for whatever is happening next.

I awaken to the true me by remembering that God holds me in high esteem. If ever thoughts of being unloved or unlovable or being incapable or undeserving come to mind, I remember how God sees me. God holds me in such high esteem, how can I think anything less of myself? How can I act as if I am anyone other than the loved and capable person I am? Remembering that I am loved by and precious to God, brings out the best in me. And when I think or interact with others, I know that they are precious and loved by God, too.

When I look at others and remember they are sacred creations of God, I can do no less than love and hold them in high esteem as well. Yes, I remember that we are all loved by God and precious to God. In that remembering, I discover the true joy of spirit.

LIFE IS A JOURNEY

Blessed are my eyes, for they are the eyes of God.
Blessed are my ears, for they are the ears of God.
Blessed is my heart, for it's best with the love of God.
Blessed is my body, for it's alive with the life of God.
Blessed is my mind, for it's filled with the intelligences of God.
Blessed am I in heart, for I am one with God's love.

At times, I may feel as if my life is a huge ship that I am trying to keep afloat as I navigate through uncharted water. However, I find much-needed relief from stress as I go within for divine direction. As I open my heart and mind to the presence of Spirit at the center of my being, I place my life into the flow of divine order that is always present.

Calm and confident, I prayerfully set my sight on a clear course. I respond to ever-present Spirit rather than react to the various outer circumstances of my life. As I do, my journey becomes effortless. Turning to God in prayer, I know that all things are possible. Following directions, I am always in my right place to recognize and accept my highest good.

Opening the doors. I confidently open the doors to my good. A door can be a symbol of freedom or of bondage; depending upon my viewpoint. Some closed doors are opened with the turn of a doorknob; others must be opened with a key; while others require only a push. When a door appears closed, some action on my part may be necessary. Faith may be needed to turn the knob, prayer may be the key to unlock the door, willingness and persistence may supply the push to open it. A door is a meaningful symbol, for it represents both leaving and entering. Some doors lead away from a phase of my life that is completed. Through others, I enter a new phase or untried path. Today, I confidently open the doors to my good.

I let go of concern and let God be God in my life. Sometimes life events lead to anxiety and worry. When I feel anxious, I take a moment to remember I am not alone. Whether I have a difficult decision to make a challenge that seems overwhelming, or even a small matter that confuses me, I can take any issue into prayer. Spirit works in unknowable ways. So in prayer, I let go of trying to control every outcome. I release my need to micro-manage every detail. I gratefully acknowledge that all is working for good. I listen for guidance and prayerfully give thanks as I receive it. Releasing my concerns, I let God be God in my life and then I do what is mine to do.

There is much to learn in life, but it is best to learn how to live. I keep on keeping on. When things get rough, as they sometimes will get in life, I may think about giving up on a dream or a goal. However, from deep within, I receive the encouragement to keep on keeping on.

I remember that God is with me, that God is ready to help me throughout every challenge, which may come my way. God loves me and He has prepared me for success. I keep faith in God and commit myself to following the guidance and inspiration that I receive. Then I begin to see challenges are opportunities for me to learn more about the true desires of my heart and myself. I keep on keeping on, and discover the joy of living my dreams!

With peace in my heart, I step forward on my life's journey. It's been said that every journey begins with a single step. Is there a step that you need to take in your life, right now? Do you need to move forward in your work? In a relationship? In my spiritual life? If the answer is yes, take that step now. My step may be opening my heart to new ideas and possibilities, looking at creative avenues of self-expressions or discovering new ways to learn, grow, and express myself as a spiritual being.

Life is a journey of small steps. Some require great courage and strength. Some only require the desire to move forward and experience something new. With each step, I enter a new experience, one that is mine alone. I take that step now.

I AM ON MY WAY

I know that the "I AM" in me is Spirit. That it is always wise, always well, and always rich. So I give up the habit of saying, "I am foolish, I am sick, I am in need." I realize the "I AM" in me is the I am of infinite being. It is that within me, which is eternal, enduring, and constant. It is that within me, which knows no change of defeat. When I say, "I am," I am not speaking of personal. I am realizing the presence of peace, wisdom, love, and life. That's "I AM."

WHAT IS YOUR FAVORITE DAY?

Monday   Tuesday
Wednesday   Thursday
Friday   Saturday
Sunday

Every day is my favorite, when I count my blessings. With God, every day is a day to begin again to trust and feel His love for me and know that in all the confusion, there is a gift to be found. With God, every day is a day to hope for the very best to believe my prayers are being heard. That good news is on its way. That anything can happen between yesterday and tomorrow. With God, every day is a day to count our blessings, to remember whose children we are, and what we're capable of, through a Father who cares so much.

55

Sundays just for me. I find deep satisfaction in doing for others, but today I take time to do something that supports my own health and well-being. Taking a few moments, I stretch before I leave the comfort of my bed. I watch sports on television, such as basketball, football, tennis, and golf. I take time to enjoy a healthy meal. I savor the pleasure of reading. At whatever time of day I pray and meditate. I find that the rest of my days unfolds in order. At peace and free from worry, I am creative in my approach to both challenges and opportunities, and I welcome the positive results. Prayer is my daily practice that strengthens my faith and enriches all that I experience.

Each day is a chance for a fresh start. Everything that happened before is in the past. I appreciate the value of the lessons I have learned, but now it is time to move on. I see each day as a new beginning. I wake up renewed and feel rejuvenated about the good that is waiting for me knowing that God is with me in whatever I do. I also know that I will be blessed by whatever I do. My day starts by thanking God for making right choices throughout the day.

I am blessed with the gifts of joy and enthusiasm. Every day can be a cause for celebration when I look at the world through my eyes of joy and happiness. I don't need to wait for a party or holiday to show my enthusiasm. Every day is a celebration in which to rejoice in the life, love, and joy. Great things are in store for me. I welcome them with eager and anticipation. Filled with enthusiasm and optimism, I give thanks for newfound opportunities. Each task becomes brighter. I feel an enthusiasm for life that a wonder-filled child would naturally feel.

With a grateful heart, I praise God for abundant blessings. My life is unfolding in divine order with the perfect timing of events and circumstances. My good is ready for me, and I am ready for good. With the blessings of answered prayers come new ideas about sharing with others. I cannot help but think of loving and passing along my good. Now in the serenity of prayers, I express my gratefulness.

> *"Dear God, with grateful heart, I praise*
> *You, realizing more each day how abundantly*
> *I have been blessed. I am thankful for each*
> *opportunity, too, and to be blessed. My*

57

*appreciation for You is continually growing.
In the joy of Your presence, in the bliss of
giving and receiving, I say Thank You, God."*

I learn and grow in every experience. If we were never challenged to adjust to new conditions and new people, we would not grow. Growth gives life zest and meaning. When I am confronted with changes, I stop and look back over my life. I see every change has brought me new knowledge. Every challenge has given me confidence and perspective. I have no reason to be hesitant or fearful about my current situation. So I approach change with my mind and heart open to receive the new knowledge, the new confidence and the new vision it will bring. Free of resistance, I welcome challenge as an opportunity for growth and development, and my life is enriched.

I live in the present moment, knowing there is time enough to do all that is mine to do. Yesterday was over. Tomorrow is yet to come. I live in the present moment, savoring its joys and learning from its challenges. The past and the future have their places, but my place is now. I choose what I want to accomplish at the present.

I know that I will always have time enough to do the

most important things, for there is always time enough for whatever I put first. I have time enough for laughter. I have time enough to be a friend and to show kindness to others. I have time enough for work and play. I have time enough to do whatever fulfills the longing of my heart. I have time enough to all that is mine to do.

We may or may not celebrate our birthdays each year, but each new day is reason enough to celebrate the gift of life. The gift of God's Spirit is within us. Through the Spirit of God within, we have the ability to achieve anything we desire. With God, nothing is impossible; nothing can keep us from experiencing the joy and fulfillment that God created us to experience.

Although we may go through what seems to be a failure, we know that it is a valuable learning experience that urges us further along the path. So we celebrate this experience and give thanks for what it has taught us about life. We grow in spiritual awareness as we let God show us what life can be. "Thank you, God, for Your wonderful gift of life!"

I give thanks for life and for the opportunity to become all that I can be (ageless). Regardless of my age, each day is an opportunity to be reborn to a life of happiness and love, and to celebrate my growing awareness of truth. HAPPY BIRTHDAY to a new me! I do not have to wait for my actual birth date life. My life is so full of blessings that every day I give thanks to God. "God, thank you for life, which energizes and restores me to wholeness, as it moves through my entire body. Thank you for the light, which shines on me and through me to those I care for. Your light shows me the way. Thank you for unlimited blessings in my life, order in my affairs, and peace in my heart. Thank you God, for the opportunity to become all that I am capable of being!" ***This little light of mine, I'm going to let it shine…SMILE!***

GIVING

I say yes to my good. The willingness to receive grows within me. Whatever good I may be seeking even more is actually avoidable. Wherever I am, whatever I anticipate, my surroundings holds blessings for me. They may be more noticeable at times than at others. Yet at every turn in my life, I look for blessings because I know they are there.

As I continue to be aware of this goodness, my blessings exceed my expectations. God is ever-present. My good is ever-present. The infinite abundance of blessings is so rich, so willingly given. It is wondrous to receive. I cannot give a blessing without receiving one in return. As I give of myself, my good come to me, heaped up, pressed down, and overflowing. An abundance of serenity, healing, order, and prosperity pour forth in my life. God gives, and I say yes to my good.

As I lend a helping hand to the people around me, I am fulfilling the law of giving and receiving. No resource is depleted when I freely give it away. Nothing is lost, but rather much is gained. By being of help to others, I am participating in the flow of life. I have knowledge, gifts, talents, and resources to share with others, and they have theirs to share with me. Together, we are partners and participants in a beautiful truth. I give freely; it may be that I will never see or experience the outcome of my gifts, but that it is of no concern to me. In helping others, I have been given an opportunity to share of my resources and myself. I have participated in the flow of life.

I give generously and receive abundantly. I am blessed in giving generously and receiving fully that I connect with the God energy in me. When I act thoughtfully towards another, I receive thoughtfulness in return. As I give love to others, I feel more fully loved. As I circulate my financial resources with joy and gratitude, I find that my life is richly blessed with experience and substance that bring me even greater joy. I give thanks for friends and loved ones, joyful activities and all the good that life offers. I give generously, receive abundantly, and life is truly blessed.

Satisfaction is not a measure of what I do, but of what I believe. I give my best effort to all that I do. I tap into creativity of ideas, the discipline of patience and compassion of understanding. I release self-criticism and judgment of others. I am everything I need to be to do my best. The words of my mind and hands and heart are a blessing. My attention is not drawn comparing what others have to what I have or don't have. I focus my attention on the plenty in my life. I am thankful and blessed with enough to have to share.

Organizations that I support financially are: Alpha Kappa Alpha (AKA), Educational Advancement Foundation, Inc., which is a foundation to provide perpetual support for life-long learning, United Negro College Fund (UNCF): *A mind is a terrible thing to waste*, and the Special Olympic Partner.

My life is enriched by the companionship of my friends and reaching out in friendship to others. I am grateful that we share our lives with one another through the happy times and the challenges. I consider new ways to support my friends; perhaps a phone call just to say,

"I am thinking of you today," or an offer to help on a project. It is my intention to reach out to each of my friends, because I find joy in giving them my time, my attention, and my *Love*.

FORGIVENESS

*A*ll that have offended, I forgive—past things, present things, and future things. I forgive, within and without, and all that has made me unhappy. I forgive. I forgive positively everyone who needs forgiveness of the past or present. I am free and they are free, too.

I forgive and live in peace. My words may not always be kind or compassionate, and, at times, I may feel hurt by the words of others. In these instances, I take responsibility for my words and actions. I participate in gentle conversations by explaining what I heard and sharing my feelings. I am a loving child of God, through my willingness to hear others, objectively. I open the door for clear, compassionate communications. I rid my own heart of negativity by speaking my love truth with love, and listening with love, as well.

With forgiveness, I help create a new, brighter day. How easy is it for me to forgive? Does it depend entirely on whom or what I am forgiving? When I understand that there is a blessing for me each time, I forgive. Forgiving self, as well as others, becomes easier. As I forgive, I give up resentment and anger, so it is really a fight that blesses me in giving it. It's not that I am supporting a negative or disrespectful behavior. I believe claiming that there are divine qualities within us waiting to be expressed in loving, helpful ways. I am an encourager, not a critic. I give others and myself the attention I would give anything or anyone I value. Forgiveness is like a sunrise that is announcing a new and brighter day.

Forgive. Each time I forgive my heart opens! Opening my heart to love, I forgive the strength to forgive. Holding on to feelings of resentment or judgment may feel safer. I may want people to change before I forgive them. But, here is another answer, allowing the indwelling Christ Spirit to open my heart to love. Through the power of Christ in me, I have the strength to release the weight of un-forgiveness. Christ's love is stronger than any perceived injury or harm. Another person's unkindness towards me has no power to hurt me. To forgive is to love, and to love is to let the Christ Spirit heal my heart and my life.

I love the life I live now. To live without regrets requires the discipline of awareness, the compassion to forgive and the courage to change. I am aware of my true nature that I am a spiritual being, loved, and guided by the divine infinite. Anytime I feel I have failed to be my best self, I remember that I am learning to live and love, at the highest level of my soul's wisdom. I ask Spirit to reveal what I might change to move closer to being my best self. I then ask for the courage to make that change. Knowing I am doing my best, I have compassion for myself. As I learn to forgive others. I am at peace with the path that has brought me to this place of understanding. I have no regrets, and I love the life I live now.

As I forgive, life lessons bring me closer to knowing the peace within my heart. When I experience a hurtful exchange with another person, I allow forgiveness to release me from the pain. Forgiving does not condone unacceptable behavior, it gives me permission to break free from the person or situations may have on me.

With compassion, I forgive myself for doing something I regret or for neglecting to do something I wish I had done. Through self-forgiveness, my capacity to forgive others increases and judgment is released. As I forgive, I gratefully accept the peace. I forgive others and hold them in prayer. When I have been hurt by another, the last thing I may feel like doing is forgiving. If a person says something that upsets or insults me, an organization takes action that angers me, or life seems unfair, there is a part of me that may want justice, not forgiveness.

In truth though, there is no victory in resentment. I am the one who suffers when I choose not to forgive. As I release and let go of my need to defend my position. I am liberated; I experience a return to peace, rather than a need to blame. While I do not condone hurtful behavior, and I take action when necessary, I do not hold anger in my heart. I forgive and bring the matter to God in prayer.

As I forgive, I remember that life is a learning experience and that the people I need and the situations I encounter are part of that experience. The lessons I learn may be tough or joyful, but each one helps me to grow...*and forgive us our debts as we also have forgiven our debtors* ~Matthew 6:12

REMEMBERING THOUGHTS

When life seems overly serious, a good laugh can change my outlook for the day to a truer, brighter perspective. A funny article, movie, or television program not only provides a distraction from concerns, it also reminds me of the absurdity of allowing outer circumstances to impede my awareness of the joy within.

A deep, hearty laugh impacts my entire being in a positive way. As I chuckle, I release tension, which allows me to view my world with a positive outlook and perceive the possibility for good that each day holds. The more I am aware of my oneness within, the more reason I have to laugh and be happy.

Through the power of laughter, I am invigorated and revitalized. How often have we been reminded,

"Laughter is the best medicine?" Doesn't it feel good to have a hearty laugh or even a gentle chuckle? When we laugh, especially if we find something very amusing, we are physically energized and invigorated. The more we laugh, the more air we take in as our lungs work harder, so does our heart pumping blood faster and revitalizing every cell and muscle of our body.

Mentally, we alleviate our mind of worry, stress or strain. All else is forgotten as our mind focuses on the humor at hand. The laughter we enjoy can also be shared with others. Through the power of laughter, we are invigorated and revitalized.

Happiness is Remembering. Happiness is much more than a pleasant effect that comes from recalling rich experiences out of our past, wonderful as that kind of happiness is. Happiness is a state of being that comes from remembering bring to mind again and keeping in mind the truth of our own divine nature. Happiness is a state of health prosperity, peace, and well-being. It is anchored permanently in the truth of our own being, in God, the Creator.

Happiness is remembering to be grateful. Happiness is remembering to praise and give thanks at all times in all circumstances. The joy of the Lord is your strength, and that joy is stirred into happiness as a reminder of whom and what you are and then extends your remembrance to your neighbor. Peace will come to the Earth as a permanent resident when all humanity remembers that God is our Father, we are His children and that all good is our heritage.

BELIEVE IN YOURSELF

BE SMART

USE YOUR BRAINS

NEVER QUIT, EXPECT TO WIN

BE READY TO GO

SMILE!! ~ SMILE!! ~ SMILE!!

You Will Never Know When Your Picture Will Turn Up

"Don't Worry Be Happy" ~ SMILE!!

"I have a pocket full of miracles for you and me" ~ SMILE!!

Veloisa Diana Simpson

*"Never let your right hand know what your
left hand is doing"*

"Reach for the moon, and you just might catch the star"

Heavenly Father, I Thank You for Loving Me.

"Think Big!!"

"What you don't learn from your parents, you

learn from the World"

Live
(Well)
Love
(always)
Laugh
(often)

"The Three L's"

~ LOOK ~

Look, you will see

~ LISTEN ~

Listen, you will hear

~ LOVE ~

Love, you will live

Keep your Friends close and your

Frienemies closer

MUSIC OF MY LIFE

(Songs in my Heart)

The songs in my heart celebrate living. What are my heart songs? They are of joy and hope, love, and beauty. Does it reflect who I am and who I want to be? The songs of my heart set the time for each day and for my living. I have a song of gratitude and thanksgiving. I choose a song of friendship. I choose a song of living. With every sound, my heart beats with joy.

"Let's Stay Together" (Al Green)

"That's What Friends Are For"
(Dionne Warwick & Friends)

FRIENDSHIP

A friend is someone who loves you,
No matter what you may have done;
A friend cries when you are saddened
And laugh when you need to have fun.

A friend walks with you on the path
Of Life, and together you share
The beauty, the strength, the wonder
Of the one that dwells everywhere!

A friend drops you hand when need be
For sometimes alone we must go;
A friend is a most precious gift,
God loves us, a friend tells us so.

*P*erhaps there is no other sign to the world that conveys friendship, love and peace in a more universally understanding way than a _SMILE_. A smile is a message of acceptance and gladness from one person to another. So, I choose to smile and let my smiles make an unmistakable statement about me. I am accepting and friendly. And the response I receive is fantastic. Friends and strangers, adults and children, from a simple facial expression of the gladness that fills me. A smile is a happy, uplifting thought that I released to shine out into the atmosphere around me. I am opening the window to my soul in order to experience the love of God that lives within me and to share that experience with others.

Throughout my life, I have countless opportunities to be a friend and to make new friends. Each friendship is an occasion to experience God in action to behold kindness, peace, happiness, and love in each person I meet. Each friendship is also an opportunity for me to reveal my highest and best qualities.

My friends and I balance one another's strengths and weakness, as we walk our life's paths. My friends know me and love me, lift my spirits by their presence, and help me find my way in the world; I gladly reciprocate. Each friend is a blessing my life. Each one has helped me become the person I am today; I thank God for my friends.

SMILE !!!

Veloisa Diana Simpson

TAKE TIME

Take time to think, it is the source of power
Take time to read, it is the foundation of wisdom
Take time to pray, it is the greatest power on earth
Take time to love and be loved, it is a God-given privilege
Take time to be friendly, it is the road to happiness
Take time to play, it is the secret of perpetual youth
Take time to laugh, it is the music of the soul
Take time to give, it is too short a day to be selfish
Take time to work, it is the price of success
Take time to do charity, it is the key to heaven

*I*n making wise choices, I make the best use of my time. At times, it appears that I need more hours, more days, more productivity to finish what is my responsibility to complete. In actually there is always enough time for what is needed. As I take a few moments to pray. Making wise choices concerning my time, energy, and perfect use of them, I apply myself willing and thoughtfully to a goal or project. I blend my commitment and dependability with my joy and enthusiasm. There is a natural sequence of time for completion. Within each day, each moment, there is enough time!

Whenever I seem to be running out of time to do what I need to do, I take a reality check. Starting with this observation: There is the same amount of minutes and hours in each day. Check! I am the master of my time because I can make a choice. Check! I have no reason to feel out of control as I look forward to the next few hours or days. Check!

I gain confidence about being the authority over my time by first starting my day with prayer. Centered and relaxed, I don't fight time; I go with the flow. I think with clarity and act efficiently. I know when to say yes and when to say no. I feel composed, and my day flows smoothly. I have time enough to do whatever it is before this day.

LEARN TO LISTEN

Listen—and you will hear. I take time to listen to what those around me are saying. I appreciate every word of encouragement, every bit of acknowledgement shared. I listen for the sound of joyful laughter or for a delighted shout of surprises. And each time I hear such joy, I offer a word of thanks to God, who has given me the ability to listen beyond the mere syntax of words. As I truly listen, I hear the unspoken need in a neighbor's voice and offer to be of help. If I see someone in distress, I offer a helping hand and words of comfort. I do my best to communicate with those who do not speak the same language as I do. And I listen to that still small voice within that is constantly reminding me that I am a beloved child of God.

I listen from my heart. I rely on my ears to hear, but my heart to listen. When someone speaks to me, I not only hear the words, but also with focused attention, I truly listen to what they are saying and the feelings they are expressing. I am an active and attentive listener, asking for clarification to help me understand. I listen this way because I know what it means to be heard.

I also listen with my heart to the messages of the Christ Spirit within. I still my thoughts and wait in the temple of sacred silence for the still, small voice. My guidance and help may come through words, feeling or as a unmistakable knowing. If I need confirmation or clarification, I ask and listen, knowing I will receive.

I BELIEVE

I believe in Jesus Christ, the Son of God,

who is Lord forever

I believe that Jesus was born of the Virgin Mary

I believe that Jesus died and rose

because of his love for me and for all people

I believe in forgiveness

I believe my true citizenship is in heaven

While in this life, I let the love of God fill all my days

and all my nights.

LIVING MY DREAM

*F*ulfilling a dream and accomplishing a goal have their own rewards. It is often the journey to the fulfillment and accomplishment. However, that satisfies the earning to learn more and to explain one's horizons. Whatever journey I am on today, I enjoy every moment of it. Every turning point is a change of direction that enriches my experiences.

I'm thankful for every lesson learned, every dream coming true. I am making the most of my time and my efforts. I make contributions of my creativity and skills, my ideas and time, and the desire to enhance the lives of others. I am preparing for my future. Dreaming of the future and setting attainable goals for me are exciting and invigorating. There is joy in envisioning what my heart desires and what I can contribute to the people. I love and the world in which I live.

In faith, I know that my future is secure. I am preparing for my future. As I enjoy making plans and setting goals, I affirm that whatever I may need or whatever good I desire is already here, right now. Just waiting for me to realize its full potential. Affirming this truth builds awareness of the activity of God in my life. I am grateful for everyone and everything.

As I awake, I take a deep, body-filling breath in and out. With each breath, I express love and gratitude for a new day and the many opportunities that await me. Gratitude and praise open the way for greater joy and richer life experiences. Appreciation fills me with vitality and enthusiasm. I feel renewed and filled with life's energy. My heart is open and receptive to new experiences, knowing that whatever comes my way. I see and feel that good in it.

As I go about the activities of my day, I feel myself swaying with rhythm of love and gratitude. I audibly say "Thank You!" as if the whole world could hear it, and I imagine it responding back to me, "You are welcome!" I experience the fullness of life because I am flexible. I never give up on my dreams or myself. When a change seems to alter my plans, I don't give in to feelings of helplessness or hopelessness.

My divine purpose is to be creative and to find fulfillment in whatever I am doing. Any tendency to be rigid in my thinking falls away as I welcome divine ideas into my awareness. Pressure or fear may threaten to derail my dreams. I eagerly move forward and experience the fullness of life with flexibility and the expectancy of good.

Dream…I have good reasons for never letting facts get in the way when I am pursuing my dreams. Facts may change, but truth is changeless. Divine inspirations are my sure, steady support in setting goals and fulfilling my dreams. I move forward to envision the possibilities of what can be. This is not careless daydreaming. I am a God inspired creative dreamer.

Divine ideas lead me in considering possibilities and in applying them in my own life. In the quiet of prayer, I feel a stirring of divine inspirations. Following my dreams, I give thanks for the good that is unfolding.

I may never see tomorrow. I may never see tomorrow, there is no written guarantee, and things that happened yesterday belong to history. I must use this moment wisely for it soon will pass away. And be lost forever, as part of yesterday. I thank God with a humble heart for giving me this day.

This is the year! This is the year that my dreams do come true, as I am blessed with life-celebrating opportunities. Expectations will flow this year from my vision of good. I am an active participant in the joy-filled life of me. This is the year that I move forward with zeal and enthusiasm, giving and receiving, committing to purposeful, rewarding goals.

This is the year that brings happiness, a year that I will live to bless. Wonderful, wonderful, fortunate me, for this is the year that my dreams come true!

This is the year!

"I Say To Myself, What A Wonderful World"

SMILE!!!